HIROSHIGE
AND
JAPANESE LANDSCAPES

TOURIST LIBRARY : *2*

TOURIST LIBRARY

Volumes Already Published

Volumes in Preparation

"Night Rain on Karasaki Pine Tree" (ref. page 91.)

HIROSHIGE
AND
JAPANESE LANDSCAPES

BY

YONE NOGUCHI, D. Litt.

JAPAN TRAVEL BUREAU
TŌKYŌ

Printed by TOPPAN PRINTING CO., Tōkyō, Japan

EDITORIAL NOTE

The purpose of the Tourist Library Series is to give the passing tourists and other foreigners interested in Japan a basic knowledge of various phases of Japanese culture. When completed, the Series is expected to include a hundred volumes or so, and will give a complete picture of Japanese culture, old and new. It is hoped that by perusing these studies of Japanese life the reader will gain some insight into the unique culture that has developed in this country throughout the ages.

Each volume in the Library is the work of a recognized authority on the subject. The present volume, "Hiroshige and Japanese Landscapes," was written by the late Dr. Yone Noguchi, who was a professor in the Keiōgijuku University, and author of the excellent treatises on wood-block artists entitled *"Hiroshige"* and the *"Six Greatest Ukiyo-e Artists."*

In publishing this revised and enlarged edition, we desire to record our sincere appreciation of the help given by Dr. Shizuya Fujikake, author of "Japanese Wood-block Prints" (Tourist Library Vol. 10) and Mr. Sadao Kikuchi of the Tōkyō National Museum, who gave us many valuable suggestions in the editing of this book. Our special thanks are due to Mr. Shōzaburō Watanabe, well-known wood-block print publisher in Tōkyō, who generously allowed us to take photographs of many color prints from his fine collection for use in this books.

THE EDITOR

May 1, 1954.

CONTENTS

ILLUSTRATIONS

IN COLOR

IN BLACK AND WHITE

NOTES

1. In the text (pages 1 to 106) all Japanese names are given in the usual Japanese manner, i. e., the surname before the given name.

2. The – signs used over o and u in Japanese words mean that the vowel sound is lengthened.

3. All the illustrations in this book, with the exception of four which were made available to us through the courtesy of the Tōkyō National Museum, were reproduced from originals belonging to the collection of Mr. Shōzaburō Watanabe.

4. In the captions of the illustrations only the names of artists other than Hiroshige are given; all the other prints are by Hiroshige.

CHAPTER I

LIFE OF HIROSHIGE

Hiroshige was born in the ninth year of Kansei (1797), when Utamaro,* a great painter of female beauty and of the harem, had just finished the work on which his present fame rests. During the régime of the eleventh *shōgun*** of that period, the times were speedily relaxing into an ephemeral epicureanism. Hiroshige's birthplace was the compound of the fire-brigades at Yayosugashi, Edo (present Tōkyō). Here, his father, Gen-emon, lived as one of the officials, who, after serving twenty-five years, resigned the post to Hiroshige when the boy was but thirteen years old. At this time Hiroshige lost his parents almost simultaneously. The work at the office must have been nothing more than nominal that even a boy of thirteen could do it, and at the same time pursue the leisurely study of art which Hiroshige had already begun. This was because the fire-brigades to which he belonged had only to attend to the *shōgun's* castle where fires occurred but seldom. Besides, although wearing two swords, people of Hiroshige's class were but small and insignificant.

---

* "Japanese Wood-block Prints" by Dr. Fujikake. Tourist Library Vol. 10, pp. 48-49.
  "Japanese Fine Arts" by Prof. Sagara. Tourist Library Vol. 9, pp. 136-138.
** Tokugawa Ienari, the eleventh *shōgun,* held office from 1787 to 1836.

Hiroshige held the post till he was twenty-seven years old, when he turned it over to Nakajirō, his son or uncle (the relationship is not certain). Leaving for good the house which Nakajirō had established, Hiroshige started independently a branch of the family in the profession of the fine arts. Before he was admitted as a pupil to Toyohiro's studio in 1812, when he was sixteen, Hiroshige had already shown his precocious talent in a scroll entitled "Procession of the Luchu Islanders," which Hiroshige had drawn from life when he was a boy of ten. This appears certain, because in 1806, according to an authentic record, the shogunate government of Edo received an official visit from an ambassador bringing tribute from the Luchu Islands. When the present writer saw this historical scroll some years ago, he was at first surprised at Hiroshige's ability, certainly remarkable for his age. Then he felt sorry that Hiroshige was obliged to suffer a restraint of twenty-five years before he could establish his name in public.

It is said that Hiroshige wished at first to become a pupil of Toyokuni* and not of Toyohiro,** but because he already had too many pupils, Toyokuni refused

---

* Utagawa Toyokuni (1769-1825) was a pupil of Utagawa Toyoharu (1735-1814). He was skilful in painting women and *kabuki* actors. In painting the latter he established a style of his own. He had many pupils, and each of these had his own followers, so that the Utagawa clan of painters dominated the *ukiyo-e* world in the later days of the Edo period (1615-1868).

** Utagawa Toyohiro (1773-1828) was also a pupils of Toyoharu. In his earlier days he concentrated on portraits of actors, but finding Toyokuni unrivalled in that field, he turned his energies to pictures of beautiful women. He made many prints and painted many excellent portraits of women.

A Bevy of Kyōto Belles Enjoying the Summer Evening on a Pier Extending over the Kamo River.   By Toyohiro

"Warrior and Man-eating Goblin." Published by Iwataya around 1819.

him. It is not without interest, however, to muse on the possible outcome had Hiroshige ever been received by Toyokuni, and duly impressed by his platitudes, if not vulgarity, in superficial arabesque-making. Of course there is nothing more foolish than to think that anything could have made a successful Kunisada* (Toyokuni the Third) of him, even though, born to a corrupt age in holiday mood, he was charmed by the stage and actors. Among the extant works of his earliest period there are found, even today, a number of actor-prints. No one would deny, I believe, the happiness of Hiroshige's association with Toyohiro,** who was not aiming at popularity, and certainly was not in Toyokuni's class, and who therefore resembled Hiroshige in temperament. Moreover, what pleased the youthful Hiroshige most, I think, was that Toyohiro never used on him his master's hammer of discipline, but watched patiently over the youth's development.

The book, "Hiroshige Wakagaki" (Hiroshige's Early Work) by Nakamura Tatsujirō, 1925, contains many female figures in "Soto to Uchi Sugata Hakkei" (Eight

---

* Utagawa Kunisada (1786-1864) was one of the ablest pupils of Toyokuni the First. In 1844 he assumed the title of Toyokuni the Third. (The title of Toyokuni the Second was taken by the adopted son of Toyokuni the First.) He produced numerous prints of beautiful women and *kabuki* actors of his time. Beside this form of art he left many hand-painted pictures, and also did illustrations for a large number of story-books known as *kusazōshi*.

** In 1812 Hiroshige became a pupil of Toyohiro. He adopted the name "Hiroshige" in the following year. His name was a combination of Hiro (廣), a part of Toyohiro (豐廣), and Shige (重), a part of Jūemon (重右衛門), Hiroshige's own name.

Views with Figures, Outdoors and Indoors) and "Goku-zaishiki Imayō Utsushi-e" (Modern Images Warm-colored), both produced about 1822. In these the influence of Eizan,* or Eisen,* is clear. But as far as the landscapes, flowers and birds are concerned, which Hiroshige produced at the time of the *Tōto Meisho* series in the Kawaguchi edition, about 1831, the influence we can trace in them is that of the Hokusai** school artists, or possibly of Eisen, since these prints of natural subjects would never have appeared under the influence of the Toyokuni school. Toyohiro was a suitable teacher to Hiroshige, if indeed he needed one at all. But as Toyohiro's student, Hiroshige was an interesting rebel, or "black sheep" who received but little direct influence from his teacher.

When Toyohiro died in 1828, Hiroshige was asked to succeed the teacher as Toyohiro the Second, but he refused with thanks, preferring to pursue his own in-

---

* Kikugawa Eizan (1787-1867) originally belonged to the Kanō school, which held the foremost position in Japanese painting in the Edo period (1615-1868). As an *ukiyo-e* painter he first followed the style and manner of Kitagawa Utamaro, but later developed a style of his own. He is the founder of the Kikugawa school of *ukiyo-e* painting.

 Kikugawa Eisen (1790-1848) was the most gifted pupil of Kikugawa Eizan. Though his work are mostly prints of women in the gay quarters, he produced some landscape prints which show his originality, and established his fame as a unique landscape artist. The "Sixty-nine Stages on the Kisokaidō" is the joint work of Hiroshige and Eisen (see page 77).

** Katsushika Hokusai (1760-1849), founder of the Katsushika school, was one of the most famous of the *ukiyo-e* artists of his time. He created a unique style in depicting beautiful women and landscapes. The "Thirty-six Views of Mt. Fuji" are his greatest masterpieces.

"Moon at Yanagibashi." Series: *Soto to Uchi Sugata Hakkei*
(Eight Views with Figures, Outdoors and Indoors).

"Waitress"—an Example of the Prints of Beautiful Women
Made by Hiroshige in his Late Years

dependent life. Although there is no complete catalogue of the work of his whole life, it is estimated by
Uchida Minoru that the total number of individual
pieces would exceed eight thousand, of which some five
thousand and five hundred pieces are color-prints, large
or small. Hence, it may be seen what a prolific painter
he was. There is reason of course to say that if his
force and energy had been used more scrupulously, he
would have become a still more distinguished artist.
Admitting that the unprincipled spirit of the time made
him produce careless work, and to repeat his subjects
again and again, Hiroshige's vitality was certainly something amazing.

I can imagine that the primary need with him was
how to pour out his lyrical mood untrameled, with his
thought about subject-matter as but of secondary importance. The same scenery appealed to him quite
differently at different times, according to the situation
and his mood. It was not that Hiroshige drew his
pictures at random on the same subject with a different
approach, but that he used the same subject when it was
diffused with a new mood or emotion. Consequently,
there are in his pictures great variations in atmosphere.
What we see in them therefore is Hiroshige's personality
and not a scenic photograph. Besides, since they are
color-prints made by hand,* one cannot expect them to

---

* "The practice in Japan had hitherto been for a publisher to
have in his employment engravers and printers, whose business it
was to cut on block and to make the impressions respectively of
the pictures painted by the artists. Thus the Edo masterpieces
of *ukiyo-e* were the work of painters, engravers and printers who

be uniform, even when they treat the same subject. The pictorial effect depends more or less on chance.

As with other artists of the *ukiyo-e* school, little is known of Hiroshige's life. Whether or not he left the firemen's compound near Yayosugashi for some other place, when he resigned his official post, is not recorded. By 1840 or 1841 he had lived in Ogachō Street, and afterwards moved to Tokiwachō Street, and still later, in 1849, to Nakabashi Kanō-shimmichi, the place where finally he died, loyal to the heart of the city of Edo. Hiroshige was fond of distant journeyings. Some of the traveling diaries he jotted down between cups of *saké* and his favourite dishes at roadside taverns (for he was a city man with epicurean tastes), remain in the "Diary of the Journey" (the major part of it lost by fire in 1923), the "Diary of the Kanōyama Temple Journey" and the "Diary of the Journey into the Provinces Awa and Kazusa," the *hokku** poems or *kyōka* (humorous *uta*** verses) which make the diaries precious.

---

gave of their energy and attention in a united effort under the able direction of conscientious publishers. Nor was that all. Lovers of art gave unstinted aid and support to the publishers in their production of works of real artistic value. In some cases, however, the color prints proved to be of inferior quality because of a lack of cooperation among the three classes of professionals, or of the fact that their publishers had an eye to their own profits, or again because of both reasons."—"Japanese Wood-block Prints," Tourist Library Vol. 10, p. 70.

* The *haiku* or *hokku*, a particularly short type of poem having but seventeen syllables. Though small in size and simple in structure, the *haiku* is not so easy to understand, still less to compare, as it may at first seem.

** The *waka* or *uta* is the principal form of Japanese poetry consisting of thirty-one syllables, without rhyme, arranged in five lines of 5, 7, 5, 7, 7 syllables.

"Cave on Enoshima Island." Series: *Honchō Meisho* (Famous Views of Japan). Published by Shōgetsudō around 1832.

Among artists of the popular school who were un-
cultured, although not actually illiterate, Hiroshige was
an exception because of his literary knowledge and tastes.
He was a man of facile pen, for in the diaries are apt
descriptions and occasional snaps of cynicism, all of
them delightful because they are casual and informal.
Had he pursued literature with the assiduity that he
espoused art, he would undoubtedly have become a
famous writer or poet. Although, as with any other
comic verses, Hiroshige's work depends upon phraseology
or puns which are ephemeral, and therefore difficult to
translate into English, the following poems from "Kyōka
Momo-chidori" will indicate his usual vein:

> *"Putting aside the moon and snow,*
> *How delightful it is to live roundly*
> *With a head more round*
> *Than a dumpling round and round!"*

The verse alludes to the common saying, *Hana yori
dango,* meaning literally "A dumpling is better than a
flower." Of course it treats with both satisfaction and
mockery the author's own shaven head. Utashige was
Hiroshige's name as a humorous poet. He sometimes
signed this name to *harimaze-e* (mixed prints of small
size) or *sensha* (also *senja*)-*fuda* (visiting cards to shrines
or temples, see the footnote, p. 82) or illustrated books
of lyrical drama. Also, some of the famous view-points
produced after 1839 bear the name of Utashige.

Hiroshige married twice. His first wife, doubtless a
typical woman, chaste and dutiful, whose sagacity as-
sisted Hiroshige to tide over many financial difficulties,

died in October, 1839, when he was forty-three. A touching story is told in the "Biographies of the Ukiyo-e Artists of the Utagawa School," by Iijima Kyoshin, that once she raised her husband's traveling expenses for sight-sketching by secretly selling her clothes and ornamental combs. It is fortunate, however, that this devoted wife knew something of the better days into which Hiroshige was slowly entering. When he took Oyasu, a daughter of Kaemon, a farmer of Niinomura village in Enshū province (the present Shizuoka Prefecture), for his second wife, is not recorded anywhere. She was sixteen years younger than her husband, and a woman of both constancy and spirit. She died on the second of October, 1876, at the age of sixty-four, having survived Hiroshige by eighteen years.

Though not always comfortable financially, Hiroshige was not exactly poverty-stricken, for in the closing years of his life he lived in a house of his own building, a presentable two-storied dwelling of five rooms. He had, however, borrowed money for it, and he worried on his death-bed over the payment of the debt. It is also hardly believable that he could not support a small family like his own when he drew, according to the estimate of Mr. Uchida, an average of two pictures a day throughout his life. But Hiroshige was careless and free in money matters, and no discredit to the Edo-man's qualification, whether proud or foolish, of "not allowing money to stay in tht pocket overnight." Again, as is seen from an extant diary in which his diet is minutely described, he was an epicure, fond of dishes not neces-

"Moon behind Maple Leaves." Series: *Tsuki Nijūhakkei* (Twenty-eight Moonlight Views). Published by Jakurindō around 1852.

sarily rich but oddly flavored. Naturally, he loved *saké*, but he was not a drunkard. Oyasu, Hiroshige's second wife, shared this taste for the cup.

Hiroshige was indeed a man wealthy in soul, though not in purse. Confirming the current dictum of olden time, he was not an Edo man "wrongly born and therefore a money-maker." Even without money he was always happy, and with unconstrained placidity he was nonchalant towards the trifling and mercenary matters of the common world. Yet he rigidly observed social courtesy. He was fond of quiet company, but treated his friends handsomely. He left these words in one of his wills, "Reduce foolish expenses without being niggardly; you should feast richly the people who kindly keep a wake before my coffin."

It must have been at the age of fifty-one, in 1847, that Hiroshige, learning from Confucian ethics* that a man should know at fifty how to resign himself to fate, shaved his head and became a novice. At this juncture Hiroshige made the third change of his personal name to Tokubei. He was called Tokutarō when he was young, and later assumed the name Jūemon. How Hiroshige may have looked with a shaven head will be seen, as Mr. Uchida pointed out in "Hiroshige," in the print entitled "Maple-viewing at Kaianji Temple, Shinagawa," one of "Famous Views of Edo" in the Yamadaya edition, 1853. Here, a shaven-headed artist is seen sketching the view by a large maple-tree in the center of the canvas. It is

---

* "At fifty, I knew the decrees of Heaven."—*Confucian Analects*, Book II, Chapter 4.

"Maple-viewing at Kaianji Temple"

amusing to think that people without knowledge of him
may have taken him for an apostate priest transgressing
the field of sketching.

Hiroshige was an artist who never thought that teach-
ing was of any value, because he used to say that the art
student should study art by himself. He was not one of
the same class with Toyokuni the Third and Kuniyoshi,* who were surrounded by pupils. Hiroshige was
of a retiring nature. Moreover, his passion for traveling
made him object to the regularity of tutorial exercise.
Yet, there were some eighteen pupils, to each of whom a
part of his name, Hiro or Shige, was given; and to seven

---

* Utagawa Kuniyoshi (1799-1861) was a distinguished pupil of
Toyokuni the First. He left many excellent prints of warriors,
and also produced landscape masterpieces which are charac-
terized by a Western style of expression.

of them, it is said, Hiroshige orally bequeathed mementos.

As he himself knew, Hiroshige was unfortunate in his pupils. Hiroshige the Second was bad. And Shigemasa, who followed Hiroshige the Second as Hiroshige the Third, was equally bad. Hiroshige the Fourth left hardly anything we can call art. After him Hiroshige's lineage ceased, even nominally.

According to the inscription on the "Memorial Portrait of Hiroshige," by Kunisada (Toyokuni the Third), and also to the preface of "Thirty-six Famous Views" published in the year following his death, Hiroshige died on the sixth day of September of the year 1858, the fifth year of Ansei, at the age of sixty-two. The disease of which he died is said to be cholera, which was fearfully prevalent in the fifth year of Ansei, according to the records of the time, and took the lives of some twenty-eight thousand people. As a man self-possessed and free, who carried life's calamity lightly, with a smile suitable to the humorous poet he was, Hiroshige found a moment amid the agonies of death to write the following *uta* poem in his usual playful vein:

> *"I leave my brush at Azuma,**
> *I go to the Land of the West**** on a journey*
> *To view the famous sights there."*

The words over the signature of Toyokuni the Third in the memorial portrait, meaning, "Shedding tears in

---

* Azuma (lit. east) is the name given to a district in eastern Japan, in which Edo was located.
** "The Land of the West" refers to the Buddhist Paradise.

Memorial Portrait of Hiroshige
by Toyokuni the Third

thought of him," express the general sentiment of the people at Hiroshige's death, and that of Toyokuni the Third, who was a great friend of the master. It is felt that Hiroshige died at the most appropriate time, because, according to the preface of "Thirty-six Famous Views" written by Shumba, Hiroshige often spoke of retiring from the art world before age and fatigue should disgrace his past. He was wise in thus knowing himself.

Supposing this memorial portrait of Hiroshige to be reliable, since the artist was his close friend, we know that Hiroshige's head, as he himself said in the verse already quoted, was as round as a round dumpling. The space between the end of the nose and the lips was long as is that of an Edo man of the older generation today. With thick eyebrows, large eyes and a high nose, his face is clear and noble. Unlike his lovely and delicate landscapes, Hiroshige's features are strong. Since he was a drinker of *saké* and a lover of fine dishes, he was portly and of a ruddy complexion.

"Yushima Shrine"—a Sketch
by Hiroshige

CHAPTER II

HIROSHIGE AND LANDSCAPES

Learned students of Japanese color-prints will be interested to know how prints of nature first lifted their small heads like aliens in the surprising growth of *genre* art, and how, finally, in the worthy hands of Hokusai and Hiroshige, they began to defy the general assumption that *ukiyo-e* art consisted of "pictures of the floating world." When those print masters of the last period realized the value of nature in the print, the original conception of *ukiyo-e* was contradicted and rejected. On the other hand, however, his revolutionary conduct may be excused if you interpret *ukiyo-e* as a synonym for *nishiki-e** (lit. brocade pictures) in general. At any rate, nature's entrance into print marked a new epoch in the printing world of Japan.

It is interesting to see that Moronobu, the very forefather of printed pictures, the sensual painter of debauchery and love, touched for a moment the landscape of a sunny coast in "Tōkaidō Bunken Ezu" (The Tōkaidō** Stations Illustrated), 1690, and preceded Hiroshige's

---

* "Japanese Wood-block Prints," Tourist Library Vol. 10, pp. 45-47.

** The Tōkaidō Highway connecting Tōkyō (formerly Edo) with Kyōto is the chief national highway in Japan. It runs for the most part along the Pacific coast. Along this highway in the Edo period there were fifty-three towns designated by the shogunate government as stage-towns and in each of these a fixed number of post-horses and coolies were regularly stationed to attend to the needs of travelers passing through.

Tōkaidō series by a hundred and fifty years. The interest of the *ukiyo-e* print, a bird's-eye view after the Western fashion, by Masanobu and Shigenaga of the middle eighteenth century, in connection with the landscapes of a later time, centers in perspective.* Most of them dwell not on an outdoor scene but on the interior of a big house, like those in the licensed quarter of Shin-Yoshiwara, or on theaters. Whether it is a crude imitation of the Hollandish engravings which drifted into the country after 1720, when the embargo on foreign books was removed, or of Chinese painting with a Western affectation which appeared in the latter half of the seventeenth century, the *uki-e* (perspective print) is interesting psychologically because it suggests how very new a logical perception was at a time when people clung to a fantastic absence of all logic.

When the youthful inspiration of Maruyama Ōkyo (1733-1795), the future master of realistic art in autographic painting, was spent during the period of Meiwa (1764-1771) in imitating perspective views, Western or Chinese, for *megane-e*** (pictures seen through a peep-box), the artistic appetite of the Edo people in general towards exoticism must have been great. How popular this peep-box was can be proved by one of Harunobu's prints in the Mutagawa series, in which two girls are seen enjoying it. It seems certain that Western invasion direct

---

* "Japanese Fine Arts," Tourist Library Vol. 9, pp. 87-89.
** *Megane-e-bako,* a "peep-box," is an apparatus in which a picture on the bottom, which is reflected on glass at the top, can be seen through a hole in one side of the box.

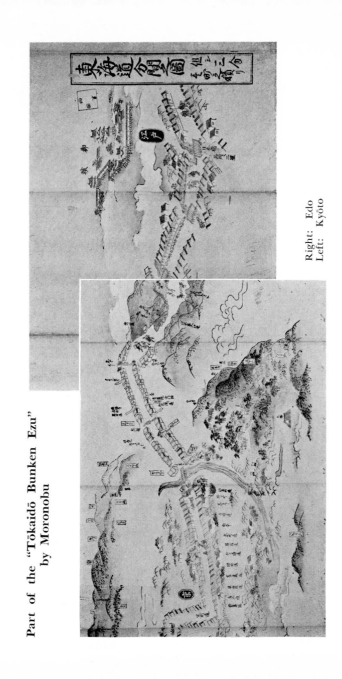

Part of the "Tōkaidō Bunken Ezu"
by Moronobu

Right: Edo
Left: Kyōto

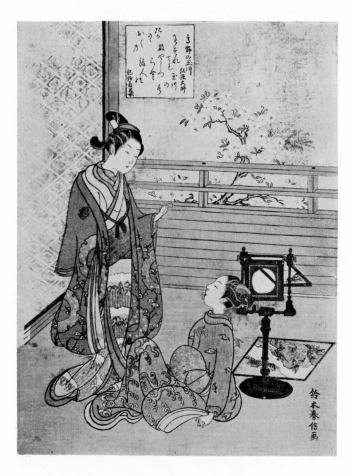

"Two Girls Enjoying a Peep-
box" by Harunobu

*By courtesy of the
Tōkyō National
Museum*

"Venice" by Toyoharu

from Holland, or indirectly through China, must have been more active in those days than now we imagine it to have been. Toyoharu (1735-1814), the legitimate successor of Masanobu and Shigenaga in the *uki-e* prints, inherited the ground Ōkyo had cultivated, and produced many prints of Western landscape in direct imitation, or through free and spontaneous imagination. Among these are a scene of Venice with gondolas afloat, and one a cathedral—perhaps in Amsterdam. But with numerous views of Edo and Kyōto, and of theater scenes, ancient battles or hunting, the naturalization of this Western technique was assured by Toyoharu.

"It seems that Kōkan's* infancy as the bogus maker

* Shiba Kōkan (1783-1818) is a disciple of Harunobu. He called

"Oyaji-jaya Park in Edo" by Kōkan

of Harunobu's prints is well atoned for by his copperplate engravings, which became inspirations or models for Hokusai's work at the end of the eighteenth century. In "Ushi-ga-Fuchi of Kudan," "Fuji seen underneath Takahashi (High Bridge)," "Great Wave at Hommoku off Kanagawa," "Benten Shrine at Haneda," and other interesting landscape-prints, Hokusai's characteristic exoticism is expressed restlessly, as is natural at a time of experiment and transition. According to his "Seiyō Gadan" (Chats on Western Art,) Kōkan began his steel

himself Harushige and painted beautiful women after the manner of his teacher. He acquired from Dutchmen the art of copperplate engraving, and published the first Japanese landscapes printed from copperplate.—"Japanese Wood-block Prints," Tourist Library Vol. 10, p. 204.)

"Ushi-ga-Fuchi of Kudan" by Hokusai

engravings in September, 1783. Although he traveled to Nagasaki, (then the only place where foreign commerce was permitted by the authorities*), from Edo, his native city, in 1778, Kōkan returned home in the following year with foreign books on art, because he could not find a foreigner there to teach him the Western technique direct. I do not know whether Kōkan was the Leonardo da Vinci of Japan, but it is no exaggeration to say that, as an enthusiastic student of Western sciences, and as a propagator of the materialism of the empiric school, he was the legitimate child of a time when the chaotic curi-

---

* "History of Japan" by Dr. Ienaga. Tourist Library Vol. 15, pp. 137-141.

"Suidōbashi in Edo"
by Denzen.

*By courtesy of the
Tōkyō National
Museum*

osity of the people was extraordinary. Before he gave
up engraving for oil-painting, it is said that Kōkan
taught his technique in engraving to Denzen.* Denzen's artistic fluency, as is seen from the number of his
extant works, qualified him as an excellent expounder of
Kōkan's method in engraving, although he was by no
means an artist of undisputed originality.

Hokusai has an imitator in Shinsai, one of his pupils,
—particularly in the artistic idiom already mentioned,

---

* Aōdō Denzen (1748-1822), also called Nagata Denzen, studied
copperplate engraving at Nagasaki. Beside reproductions of
foreign copperplate masterpieces, he himself produced many
masterpieces. —"Japanese Wood-block Prints," Tourist Library
Vol. 10, p. 199.

"Kujū-kuri Beach" by Hokuju

"Ushi-ga-Fuchi of Kudan," and others. In some of the Edo views Shinsai also followed his master with such success that a careless judge sometimes mistakes his work for that of Hokusai. There is also Hokuju, another pupil of Hokusai, who, like Shinsai, found his first inspiration in the master's foreign manner and Westernized mental attitude, and continued in it faithfully, even when Hokusai underwent a striking metamorphosis in the glory of "Thirty-six Views of Fuji," 1833. Now, the master left all the poor walkers behind, and alone climbed to the peak of creation. It is by Hokusai's magic hand that Western characteristics of landscape art, for which artists in the past had sought with passion and curiosity, now became fused into a new synthesis. When the organic coherency of landscape art was accomplished by Hokusai, people at once stopped talking about the *uki-e* prints or steel engravings of perspective views, which had alternately pleased and bewildered them during the previous fifty years.

But who is to blame if appetites grow jaded with eating and crave something new? People who had been too highly exhilarated by Hokusai's fire or novelty in shapes and colors, with which he interpreted the drama of mountain and water, now wished to settle down to twilight for a moment, indeed to the wonderful moment when nature's passion suddenly subsides. When Hokusai gave his place to Hiroshige, who was thirty-seven years his junior, the attitude of the people towards his series of Tōkaidō landscapes in 1834 was enthusiastic. Fully acclaimed with cheers and applause, Hiroshige extinguished the temporary light of Eisen's landscapes; and Kuniyoshi was wise enough to retire into warrior pictures, where he extended his stout arm in artistic bravery, finding that to contend with Hiroshige in the wrestling-ring of landscape art was at best nothing but a waste of time.

Indeed, Hiroshige's entrance into the actual field marked the climax and the conclusion of landscape art of old Japan in print. Not only the landscapes of the popular school, but also *nishiki-e* prints in general, ended with Hiroshige's death, leaving in one's mind the memory of a seven-colored rainbow which had risen from a wooden block to respond to an artist's delicate breath. With a new age in Japan lighting the horizon, it is sad

"Hodogaya," one of the "Thirty-six Views of Fuji" by Hokusai

that, like Shelley's guitar without Jane, wood-blocks, once so eloquent and responsive, became suddenly mute. Alas, one more fairyland of art is lost! Where are the artists whose magic touch can turn a block of wood into a violin of most delicate tone! Where is the amorous whisper of life in nature which they taught prints to speak?

Since the *nishiki-e* prints of Japan were originally a sensual chronicle of the manners and customs of the time, the landscape artist, Hokusai, Hiroshige and the others, were certainly rebels or traitors. It is a sad irony that the arch-traitor, Hiroshige, rang the knell for the passing of prints.

But I am happy to think that flowers, moon and

snow, real in Japan, are equally real flowers, moon and snow in the West. Therefore the work of Hiroshige, true in Japan, must be equally true, even at the center of the Western world, in England or France. I am sure that among the mountains and rivers of any Western country our Hiroshige will be found, hidden under the surface. Again, I am sure that as we are in a sense all Hiroshiges, even in the West there must be many people who would be pleased to identify themselves with this artist. A time may come when the other *ukiyo-e* artists will be forgotten in the West; but Hiroshige's name, surely, will be as lasting as nature.

Whenever I dwell on a Western landscape painting as the product of its environment, but lacking in a certain abstraction, and in the quintessence of art, Hiroshige's work comes to my mind by way of contrast, for in it the individual aspect of nature is suddenly seen isolated from the entire. His art is a thing that appeals to an artistic person in a moment of rare but sweet union with nature. In another essay I said: "It is my opinion that a true landscape artist should see a natural phenomenon at a striking moment when, being isolated, it flatly refuses to move and act in uniformity with other phenomena. Hiroshige's famous pictures, without exception, transmit and convey those rare phases which nature reveals in her blessed isolation. Following a cardinal principle of architecture, viz. concentration, Hiroshige discarded offhand all the extraneous details which are apt to blur or weaken the central theme. His handling of this secret is marvelous, although I

Flight of "Wild-Geese
at Katata" by Shinsai

know that it belongs not alone to Hiroshige in the world
of Oriental art. At any rate, he is extremely suggestive
at his best. Western landscape art, whether it is better
or worse than the photograph, usually attempts to imitate nature or to make a copy; therefore the artist may
become a soft-voiced servant to nature, but not a real
lover who truly understands her inner soul, as Hiroshige
does. A good landscape artist of the West might become
a theoriser of pigments, or something of a metaphysician
with his paint brush, or a eulogist of pigment-poems.
But since he is often bound by common circumspect
knowledge, and seldom escapes from his old habit of
expressing some meaning or purpose, it is natural that
he should fail to create a poetical landscape where real

life is nothing but suggestion. Enter into nature, I should say, and forget! Again, depict nature and forget it!"

Any suggestive art should have its own idiom of expression at once vivid and simple. I should say that every picture I see of Hiroshige at his best, seems to be new and impressive, and that the last one is always so surprising as to leave my mind incapable for the time being of an apprehension of his others. It is certain that one picture of his is quite enough, just as one picture of any other great artist of the world is enough for us. That is proof of Hiroshige's greatness.

Am I to be blamed as a vague critic, if I say that any artist, whether he be idealist or realist, is good when he is true to himself? It is true, I believe, that even a seemingly realistic work, when it is rightly executed, is always subjective; and a good picture, although superficially it may appear idealistic, is always a work that does not forget the importance of realistic expression. Hiroshige may be called a realist or an objective artist, since the artistic mood is slowly but steadily led to trees, rivers and mountains through his expression of the relation between nature and men. But who can declare that he has followed nature only superficially? It is obvious that the realistic elements of his art rendered a most important service in bringing out distinctly that indefinable quality which is often called atmosphere or pictorial personality. I think, therefore, that Hiroshige is more truly an idealist or subjective artist.

After all, Hiroshige's work, in so far as it concerns

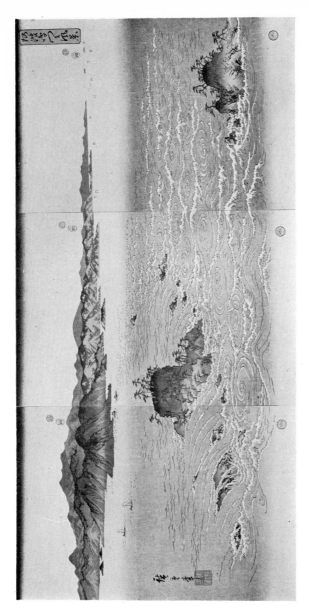

"Whirlpools at Naruto in Awa Province." Ōban Triptych.
Published by Tsutaya in 1857.

"Night View of Kanazawa in Musashi Province"

itself with landscapes and other natural subjects, is an affirmation of our old conception of art, although in most cases he recognized nature in union with humanity and found it richer among the lower classes. Unlike the masters of "mountains and rivers" in the autographic painting of Japan, who praised nature for its own sake, Hiroshige humanized it and made it speak our human tongue. I should like to know where there is any art equal to that of Hiroshige; like a living thing, nature to him, to use Whistler's classic remark, is "creeping up a bit" with a special movement, and yet conforms to Hiroshige's idiom. Once, many years ago, when I awoke to a sudden enthusiasm for Hiroshige, I began a little essay with the following words:

"In the late afternoon of a day in April, some fourteen or fifteen years ago, when greatly troubled by modern life in the West and eager to gain a true sense of perspective towards nature, I glided down the flower-reflecting water near Mukōjima, with two or three others like myself, in a 'cherry-viewing boat.' I confess that I was seeing everything through my Westernized blue eyes, and even cursing Japan for degenerating into a meaningless and foolish imitation of the West. But then seeing the calmly-settled deep blue of this Sumida River whereon we were gliding, and thinking that it was the very blue of an old Japanese color-print, my Western blue eyes suddenly changed, and I began again to look through the black eyes of a Japanese. Unlike Western blue pigment, which is often mixed with other colors to show life in action, that of the Japanese color-prints is highly homogeneous, and therefore a color as it was before any other color was mixed with it. Thus baptized by the blue of the Sumida River in the late afternoon of that spring day, I ceased at once to be a Westerner, and my mind entered slowly into the pictorial domain of Hiroshige.

"How many pictures Hiroshige drew with the Sumida River as his subject! Before my imaginative eyes, many of his pictures depicting the river in snow or under cherry blossoms, appeared as if thrown there by a magic lantern. When I thought of a particular one, 'Sumida-gawa Hanazakari' or 'Cherry Blossoms by Sumida River,' this very Mukōjima colored faintly but beautifully by the blooming cherry blossoms began to appear to me just like that picture by Hiroshige. I could not help exclaiming in spite of myself, 'Why, nature does imitate art as Wilde once exclaimed, — the Mukōjima of today imitates Hiroshige's picture of olden time!'

"As we glided through the delightful sights by the river which Hiroshige loved so dearly, and painted in so many pictures, we argued, discussed and expanded on the recent artistic advance of the human mind. There is no doubt that as our minds are glad to imitate the rare and good in art whenever they see it, you will agree, I am sure, that it is not strange that my mind, when so full of Hiroshige's pictures, could not see the views before my eyes as other than the pictures of Hiroshige. It is not true that 'the Mukōjima of today imitated Hiroshige's picture of olden time;' the fact is that my own poor mind was imitating Hiroshige's art. In other

"Sumidagawa Hanazakari"

By courtesy of the Tōkyō National Museum

words Hiroshige, hitherto unknown in my mind, awakened suddenly. Or, to use another expression, my friends and I become one with the artist who was called Hiroshige,—just as it is said that we are all Hamlets, whether men or women. As we were already all Hiroshiges, we were naturally moved by him and could react to his work as to our own creations. A Hiroshige hidden in our own minds found a representative artist in the real Hiroshige who was born in 1797 and died in 1858. He is, in truth, one of the best native and national artists of Japan."

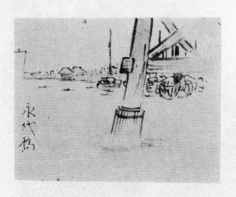

"Eitaibashi Bridge"—a Sketch
by Hiroshige

CHAPTER III

NOTES ON HIROSHIGE'S
MASTERPIECES

Different Sizes of Color-prints

Ōban, the standard size of Hiroshige's prints, is roughly 15 by 10 inches and may be either lateral or vertical.

Kakemono-e is a diptych where the top of a vertical print is joined to the bottom of another vertical sheet, making a picture 30 by 10 inches. This print is also called *nimaitsuzuki.*

Ō-tanzaku is a sheet measuring 15 by 6.6 inches. It is about the same size as the *ōban hoso-e* which was the term used before Hiroshige's era.

Triptych is a three-sheet print formed by joining the three *ōban* usually in vertical form.

"Reading a letter under the mosquito net by the light
of the paper lantern"   By Utamaro

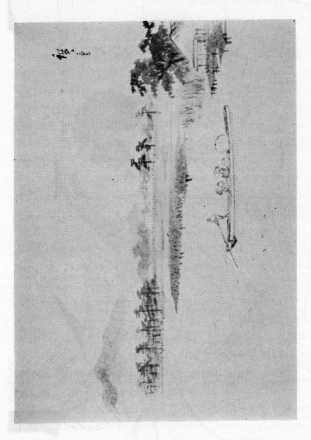

Uchiwa-e (a Black-and-White Painting
for a Fan) by Hiroshige

1. Snow Gorge in Upper Stream of Fujikawa. *Kakemono-e.* Published by Sanoki. About 1842.

I always think that the color-prints of Japan had at least two occasions when they revealed their technical excellence. One was the time they appeared with mosquito nets as pictorial property; the other was the occasion of snow scenes. Mosquito nets minutely carved, in sea-green color, are delightful indeed. I know that even the work of Kunisada (Toyokuni the Third), when composed with them, is not without a charm and beauty that make us forget his poor handling of the figures. Where is there another example of art like Hiroshige's prints of snow scenes, I should like to know, in which a technique, simple almost to the extreme, works such amazing magic? "Snow Gorge in Upper Stream of Fujikawa," the print supposed to be the companion piece of "Monkey Bridge in Moonlight," is the best example of them. Although the artist adapted to it a certain method from the landscapes of the "*Nanga* (Southern) school,*" the work is quite effective on account of the printing technique clearly used to advantage. Not depending so much on pigments, it has, I should say, a certain advantage over the Monkey Bridge print.

Of course this magic should be attributed to the cleverness of carvers and printers. I know a few examples of Hiroshige's hand painting in snow that fail to impress one as effectively as those in the prints. And when we see that the artistic effect of "Snow Gorge in

---

* "Japanese Fine Arts," Tourist Library Vol. 9, pp. 106-121.

"Monkey Bridge
in Moonlight"

"Snow Gorge in Upper
Stream of Fujikawa"

"Kameyama"

Upper Stream of Fujikawa" is differentiated according to its condition of printing, we can realize that the final technique of making a print flat or solid, rich or poor in expression, rested with the printer.

2. Kameyama. Ōban. Series : Fifty-three Stages on the Tōkaidō*. Published by Hōeidō. About 1834.

"Kameyama" is also a noteworthy specimen of Hiroshige's snow scenes, in which the artist simplified the reality of the place even to the final point of symbolism. Hiroshige's attitude in "breaking off from reality while keeping in touch with it" is clear in this work. He drew the two large parallel lines diagonally across the canvas into which he put all the things he wished to express; the space beside the lines, of course, is not merely a blank or nothing. Now the travelers on horseback or in palanquins climb up among the pine trees towards the Kameyama Castle; the sky is limpid after the fall of snow. The time is morning since the aerial space at the lower left by the mountain is evidently colored by the reflection of the sun. As far as the eye can see, the scene is purified by the snow of last night.

3. Kambara. Ōban. Series : Fifty-three Stages on the Tōkaidō. Published by Hōeidō. About 1834.

This work has a distinction among Hiroshige's snow landscapes, because it is the only one he drew of snow at night. It is said that the one with a black gradation

---

* Tōkaidō: see the footnote on page 21.

in the background, upwards from behind the houses and hills, is of the later printing, but I should say that the print in that form would be better fitted to the expression of nocturnal solitariness. I found that once when I was shown an example of the first printing, almost as stiff as freshly-printed paper money, the contors of the houses and hills that cut into the sheet gave an impression of too great a rigidity and reserve. I take a delight in prints that are in the secondary state of preservation as well as of printing.

The precipice that makes a triangle with the sloping road, the houses and hills desolately standing behind and almost buried under heavy snow, compose a scene that is not so emphatic as other famous works. But it becomes a prominent work because Hiroshige's print gives one a feeling almost akin to that of suffocation. The subject is so common that we might find it in any village of Japan. There is neither voice nor sound in the work; the two figures with candle lantern (called *odawara chōchin*) and *saké* (Japanese wine) bottle are seen moving in the opposite direction to a figure under a paper umbrella, but the heavy snow makes their walking distressed. We are glad that, meeting on equal terms with the intention and the effect the artist entertained and realized, we can enjoy the work without any forced endeavour.

"Kambara"

"Asukayama in Evening Snow"

4. Asukayama in Evening Snow. Ōban. Series:
Eight Views of Environs of Edo.
Published by Kikakudō. About 1838.

This is a most attractive composition. The snow-covered trees, small or large, arranged in orderly or disorderly array, are in delicate relation with the falling snow. The heavy coating in whitewash, with the shaded black of the background, gives the work a statuesque sense of distinct perspective. The boundary line between the road and the hill is fine at the right side of the sheet, showing the hill in the shape of a triangle upside down. Though somewhat lacking in pictorial focus or strong point of emphasis, the work strangely misses being slipshod or commonplace.

5. Evening Snow on Mount Hira. *Ōban*. Series: Eight Views of Ōmi. Published by Hōeidō and Eisendō. About 1844.

The question, which of the two, the present print or "Kameyama" of the Tōkaidō series, is the better, cannot be settled until the relative value of morning and evening is decided. The crepuscular dusk in grey and black, that is seen approaching in "Evening Snow on Mount Hira," cannot hide the indigo blue in the water lapping the mountain's feet, as the village is still full of light under the reflection of heavy snow. Adopting the traditional technique of autograph-painting, the shadowy creases of the mountains, I should say, rightly add to the work a good pictorial tone. The back mountain, perfectly white, looks so cold against that lightly shaded in black. The clear transparency permeating the work raises it to an unsurpassed position among Hiroshige's snow scenes.

6. Gion Shrine in Snow. *Ōban*. Series: Famous Views of Kyōto. Published by Kawaguchi Shōzō. About 1834.

The stone fences extend to the left and right from the large stone *torii**-gate in the center; the faint blue in the stones that matches well that of the background and foreground, presents a visionary scene, soft and harmonious, into which a sensitive mind will be easily

---

* *Torii* is a kind of portal which symbolizes Shintoism. Every Shintō shrine has *torii* (see "Japanese Architecture," by Dr. Kishida, Tourist Library Vol. 6, pp. 41-43).

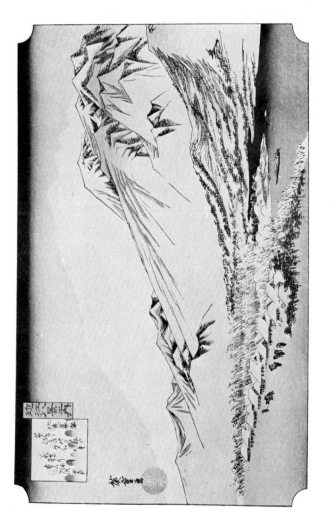

"Evening Snow on Mt. Hira"

"Gion Shrine in Snow"

immersed. Besides, there are in the print lines in various forms, straight or curving, stiff or limp, in which the cleverness of the carver's knife is beautifully expressed. And when one sees the female figures, evidently professional women and tea-house maids, dressed in green, purple, vermillion and yellow, standing by the *torii*-gate, one will not easily forget these figures in dolldom.

7. Snowing in Precincts of Kameido Shrine. *Ōban*. Series: Famous Views of the Eastern Capital.* Published by Kikakudō. About 1833-1835.

The motive and quality of the work, fresh and substantial, bring it back to a time even before that of the Tōkaidō series. At any rate, the series containing the present print, "Snowing in Precincts of Kameido Shrine," was Hiroshige's first work in the Edo landscapes in *ōban* size, which he worked on with affection during the following twenty years. This work, in twenty-one prints, is different from the others in the placing of the title, because that of each print is put out on the border in a little upright *tanzaku***-shaped tablet.

In point of real loveliness this work cuts a figure among the views of Edo, chiefly because the falling snow, not a freezing thing but a phenomenon for purify-

---

* Edo was sometimes called the Eastern Capital as the shogunate government was established there, and because it was located to the east of Kyōto, the seat of the imperial court, and the real capital of the country.
** *Tanzaku* is a rectangular strip of paper for writing poems on, usually measuring about 1 foot 2 inches by 2 inches.

ing the world, tenderly covers the drum-shaped bridges, house-roofs and trees. The bridges, stone lanterns and red Japanese apricot trees that form one line across the pond, join with another line running horizontally, in which the ornamental temple gate in red ochre stands. Making a good contrast with the pond water in blue, this strong color of red ochre breaks the general tone of grey which the white snow generously spots. The gown of a Shintō priest who crosses the bridge with an umbrella is of reddish yellow.

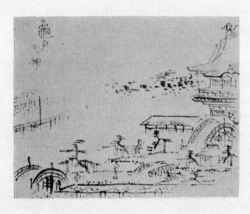

"Kameido Shrine"—a Sketch
by Hiroshige

"Snowing in Precincts of Kameido Shrine"

"Kiso Mountain in Snow"

8. Kiso Mountain in Snow. *Ōban.* Triptych. Published by Tsutaya. 1858.

Finally, in his closing period, Hiroshige brought out a snow-scene triptych in "Kiso Mountain in Snow." As one of a set of three, "Snow, Moon and Flower," the work was published by Tsutaya, 1858. Once I wrote of this print: "I would suggest that, as in looking at one of Whistler's landscapes, you step back some ten steps, slowly raise your face, and then listen to the music which the white of the mountains and the blue of the water sing in chorus, I should like to know where there is such clear silver-like poetic music as that which we feel in the arrangement of white and blue which Hiroshige's simple technique often creates accidentally. Like the pictures to which Whistler gave such names as 'Arrangement in White and Black' or 'Harmony in Grey and Green,' Hiroshige's numerous landscapes are merely arrangements of a limited number of colors, but their value is only understood by him who can hear their inner music. When I see such a work that arouses my enthusiasm, my imagination opens at once to his undying lyric voice."

Of course there are many poor prints in later editions of this work to which such a eulogy as the above would be unfitted. We must realise how the pictorial impression of a print may be changed by the manner of a printer, for the responsibility of this silent partner to an artist is certainly great. This is particularly true in a print such as "Kiso Mountain in Snow," which depends upon the color contrast of indigo-blue, white and black. The mountains under the snow are almost like a huge Chinese yam, a shape which we see so often in the landscapes of the Southern school in our auto-graph-painting. The gloominess of a snowy sky is expressed by the blue mixed with black, and the valley stream below, a greyish indigo, is never touched by the din and bustle of the world. But there are also figures and houses in the scene, suggesting that even the coldness of wintry mountains cannot entirely kill humanity.

9. Twilight Moon at Ryōgoku Bridge. *Ōban*. Series: Famous Views of the Eastern Capital. Published by Kawaguchi. About 1831.

This Edo series in the Kawaguchi edition with the famous pieces, "Twilight Moon at Ryōgoku Bridge" and a few others, that first decided Hiroshige as the artist of nature, was produced about the second year of Tempō (1831), when Hiroshige was old enough to be his own master. A few years previous to Hiroshige's appearance with landscapes, Hokusai, the "Old Man Mad about Painting*," finished carving his life's great epitaph in the series of "Thirty-six Views of Fuji." The series of "Shika Shashinkyō" (Living Images of Poetry) or "Luchu Islands," that must have decorated the shop front, side by side with Hiroshige's landscapes of this "Eastern Capital," included works of meager feeling, artistically dried up, the subjects treated being alien to

---

* Hokusai called himself *Gakyō Rōjin* (*ga* meaning painting, *kyō* mad about, *rō* old and *jin* man), and used this name on several of his works.

"Twilight Moon at Ryōgoku Bridge"

the popular mind. People also felt unsympathetic towards the landscapes of Eisen, wanting as they were in direct spirit and lacking in freshness, because of the mere transplanting of traditions into print. They must therefore have been moved and excited with an impression, so to speak, as of rain in time of drought, when they first saw this series, "Famous Views of the Eastern Capital." First of all, the subject pleased them greatly, since they were all the familiar places to which they were deeply attached, according to the season or their whim.

One who believes with me that art ascends unaided by structural expression, would be glad to see here the technique, probably an accidental phenomenon even the artist himself did not foresee, that is just crude enough to invigorate the inner spirit of the work. Hiroshige's crudity in this series is a thing that broods, working its own wild mystery, and therefore it is not undeveloped childishness at all but of riper years' in his craft.

It goes without saying that "Twilight Moon at Ryō-goku Bridge" is one of the best among the ten works of the series, if not the best of all. I have a poem, "The Man Sitting Down," which runs:—

> *"The man standing erect, sees nature upward,*
> *from paunch to head....*
> *Doubtless, a few feet nearer the stars. What*
> *in the world profits him that?*
> *The man sitting down, praised be God, sees*
> *the low garden in humble content."*

If one wishes to see Hiroshige, a man sitting down,

he should come to "Twilight Moon at Ryōgoku Bridge," in which, with all love and gratitude, the artist sees nature's loins or feet. Hiroshige is content to sit nearer the ground, because there is no need to bend his body, thanking God or praising the moon behind the bridge.

The large autumnal moon is slowly rising among the disordered clouds, to brighten up again the Sumida River, over which many bridges in evening already cast their dusky mantle. The soul of the artist that is adjusted in solitude would pay attention to nature's changing; in the moment when he thought he was part of nature, he would find himself, I believe, stepping aside some ten steps, and, if he were a Whistler, adjusting his monocle properly and scrutinizing her objectively. Hiroshige is a poet with a paint brush.

"Ryōgoku Bridge"—a Sketch
by Hiroshige

10. Autumn Moon over Tamagawa River. Ōban. Series: Eight Views of Environs of Edo. Published by Kikakudō. About 1838.

Unless one is gifted in sensibility toward the particular sweet and mellow beauty of autumnal nature in Japan, "Autumn Moon over Tamagawa River" of the series, "Eight Views of Environs of Edo," about 1838, one of Hiroshige's best moonlight views, that glimmers with something, half joy half sorrow, will not be understood by him. It is so delightful in the autumn of Japan that we can leave behind our objective attitude to create a psychological state of contemplation. Because the other seasons are too tumultuous or too stern, and prevent our observing nature minutely and appreciating her beauty accordingly, autumn is the only time when we can build a spiritual extra-territoriality in our minds where nature and life embrace each other in one song. If the print "Autumn Moon over Tamagawa River" is great, I think it is simply because the artist is highly self-possessed and beautifully composed through the virtue of lying close to the ground and listening to each delicate voice the autumnal moonlight night speaks to him. It is said of a poet that being given no identical nature, he enters into something else and fills himself with it. It is true in this moonlight view that Hiroshige entered nature empty-handed and then filled himself plentifully with the beauty it offered him. Once in my essay I dwelt on the poetical blessing of having no individuality, because individuality, often dangerously insistent and sometimes cruel like a sword, would

"Autumn Moon over Tamagawa River"

be useless in a fairy world of nature where gratitude is our one mental possession. I am glad that in "Autumn Moon over Tamagawa River," at least, Hiroshige accepted in adoration all that the mystical enchantress whispered into his innocent ears.

My delight in this piece is that, being free from a passion hackneyed and outworn, the artist sings his song most humbly in an undertone, and proves that his receptive mind is in flawless harmony. It is clear that Hiroshige understands his own mind when he understands nature; so this print, "Autumn Moon over Tamagawa River," is a psychological expression through landscape in which objectivity and subjectivity blend. I know that we Japanese are apt to become sad in autumn, a prey to the old traditional pessimism because of all that disfigures nature, and we often give ourselves to the sentimental pastime of tears. But when Hiroshige presents a good picture with legitimate sentiment, a "sentimental landscape without sentimentalism," I know that he accepted nature's decorative beauty as God revealed it to him in the moonlight of autumn.

I should like to know where there is another piece that can compete with this work, I mean the moonlight view of Tamagawa, in which autumn, wrapped in nocturnal light, steps softly from dream to dream. The moon, like a silent nun at a wake, watches through the silken mist over the fishermen engaged in night work; the willow-trees with which breezes play droop their long branches to the surface of the river, where not even one imperfection is visible. The low mountain ranges in the background are just going to sleep, saying good-night to the moon who is now quite high in the sky.

This print is certainly a gem, not only of the series, "Eight Views of Environs of Edo" but of Hiroshige's whole work, and it shows him at his highest creative power.

"Chiyogasaki"—a Sketch
by Hiroshige

11. Bow Moon. Ō-tanzaku. Series : Twenty-eight Moonlight Views.
Published by Jakurindō. About 1832.

Some years ago, I said, dwelling on a rhythmic performance or balance-making, which is one aspect of
Oriental art: "You speak of the Greek word *strophe*
from the point of emphasizing the important element
of circular swing or return. Very well. If you can
interpret this *strophe* as an obvious effort at balance or
stressing in the sense of contrast, I should say that
Hiroshige fully practised it in his best landscape prints.
Now take the piece generally called 'Bow Moon.' The
slender moon, white in entrancing ecstasy, is seen climb-
ing up from between the crags, to borrow a phrase from
the poem by Arthur D. Ficke, 'straying like some lovely
bride through the halls of Kubla Khan.' How well
balanced is this new moon with the leaping torrent
below. And what a pictorial contrast in the walled
crags on either side, with the ghostly pilgrim of heaven
between. Yet again, how the Chinese poem inscribed
on the top of the print maintains the balance with the
artist's signature below on the left."

Putting aside such technical terms, let me think
of the beauty of the work in which nature's femininity
exhausts itself. Doubtless this landscape is imaginary,
since the inscription, poor in language as in sentiment,
vaguely mentions the "morning moon flying among the
trees, and the autumnal river by the hills." If I had
been the artist, however, I should have something more
precise for the inscription. But touched by the lone-

"Bow Moon"

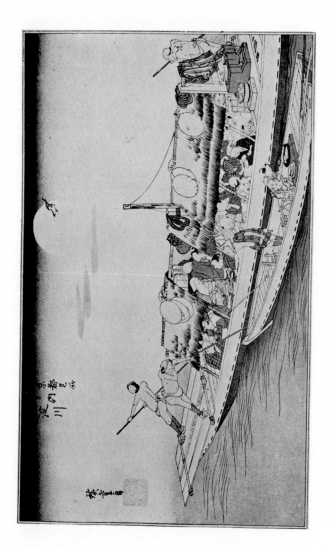

"Yodo River in Moonlight"

liness well expressed in this work I am moved strongly by its reality that, like a pearl, sparkles inwardly. We know that nature is lovely when absorbed in solitude. No one is seen on the net-made bridge which seems to be made out of fragments of a spider's gossamer web, hanging high between the crags.

12. Yodo River in Moonlight. *Ōban*. Series: Famous Views of Kyōto.
Published by Kawaguchi Shōzō. About 1834.

This is one of the most interesting prints, for it is typical of Hiroshige's art in successfully uniting nature and humanity. The moon floods the water with its beauty where the little world of plebeian people congregate in a boat in a different mood, but with life's equal purpose of enjoying their own delight. The boat was commonly called *kurawanka,* (Won't-you-eat-something boat), because, as in the print, the river hawkers waylaid the greedy passengers, shouting "Won't you eat something?" It is pleasing to notice that Hiroshige accepted here all the actualities with no irony. He must have been delighted, I imagine, when he found that the woman with a nursing baby, the pilgrim with the usual mask of a *tengu* (long-nosed, winged goblin), and happy drunkards busy in exchanging their cups, common sights he had seen in the by-streets, were miniatured in the boat, now gliding up-stream where old romances flow in emerald blue. In the sky the full moon whispers her secrets to the passing cuckoo. While busily punting on the prow, the naked boatmen alone hold, as it seems,

the mystery and beauty of the summer night that will
soon pass away.

13. Seba. Ōban. Series: Sixty-nine Stages on the Kisokaidō.[*] Published by Kinjudō. About 1835-1841.

None can deny the value of "Seba" as one of Hiroshige's masterpieces. It differs from the other pieces
in the scent and atmosphere natural to the place, which
is gloomy and damp. Though somewhat heavy and
restless, this moonlight view can challenge "Autumn
Moon over Tamagawa River" which is clear and serene.
The exquisiteness of "Seba" shows that the place is
not yet sufficiently humanized; the rustic quality carries
freshness and even poignancy.

As an artist who seldom relies on materials, Hiroshige merely used as pictorial properties in "Seba" a
raft and a brushwood boat, the moon amid the darkish
clouds and a few willow-trees that are tossed by the wind
along the nondescript country stream, thick in reeds.
These simple materials are sufficient for Hiroshige to
complete a work of great breadth and solidity, through
which his artistic personality, shadow-like but clear, is
visible to the spiritual eye.

The series of "Sixty-nine Stages on the Kisokaidō"
is a joint work of Hiroshige and Eisen (see, the foot-

---

[*] Kisokaidō (also called the Nakasendō) is an old highway which,
like the Tōkaidō, links Tōkyō (formerly Edo) with Kyōto. The
Tōkaidō for the greater part skirts the sea coast, while the Kisokaidō extends through the mountainous districts of central
Japan.

"Seba"

note, page 6). It was not, however, a case of collaboration with mutual understanding, because Hiroshige was induced to enter the field when Eisen left it. Hiroshige drew forty-seven scenes of this alternative route between the two capitals, Edo and Kyōto, against twenty-two by Eisen. With a few exceptions, Eisen's work was only worthy in technical versatility, unenlightened by artistic vision. Eisen is not quite clear in his points of emphasis; because of his carelessness in treatment, we cannot expect from him transparency or unity.

Although the Kisokaidō has not the attraction of Mount Fuji with its coils of cloud, or of the procession of handsome lords, it is not without a distinction, peculiar to the region, uncouth but humane, of which Kaibara Ekiken (also called Ekken, 1631-1715), an eminent Confucian scholar, tells rightly in "Kisoji no Tabi" or "The Journey by the Kiso Road." Here, moved by the joyous song of pack-horse drivers, even the pulse of an overwhelmingly cold nature would be quickened; the water of a valley or snow-clad stones by a mountain could not help arousing echoes in the human heart of a traveler making toward the city in the distance. Such an aspect of nature, lonely enough and not without humanity, certainly appealed to the poetical sympathy of Hiroshige, whose subtle rendering of aerial perspective and homely atmosphere, at least in some ten pieces that we choose from among the forty-seven he drew for the set, "Sixty-nine Stages on the Kisokaidō," is impressive and unique.

14. Nagakubo. Ōban. Series: Sixty-nine Stages on the Kisokaidō. Published by Kinjudō. About 1835-1841.

The long straight wooden bridge, crossing the sheet horizontally, is the center of the present composition; the traveler on horseback preceded by a pack-horse man, and the farmer carrying loads on a pole, are in silhouette as in a dream, and harmonize well with the silhouette-like forest seen in the distance below the bridge. The water in indigo blue gradation seems flooded with the blessing of moonlight. The huge, shapely pine tree by the water in the foreground dominates this visionary scene and bids the moon not to mount any higher.

Children are found playing with the dogs outside. The pack-horse man is leading a tired horse. He has ably accomplished his day's work, and may be full of joy in the anticipation of seeing his children soon at home.

There is another design of the print in which the distant forest behind the figures on the bridge is missing. It is said that the edition in this design is a later one.

**15. Night Rain at Azuma-no-Mori. Ōban. Series:
Eight Views of Environs of Edo.
Published by Kikakudō. About 1838.**

Instead of the summer rain of "Shōno," the scene of "Night Rain at Azuma-no-Mori" is of a spring rain in the night, a nocturnal caller to the trees and grasses in an undertone of lyrical song. Nature, that is re-

"Nagakubo"

"Night Rain at Azuma-no-Mori"

leased from the cruel hand of winter, is bidding a final farewell to the bleakness that still faintly hangs over the scene. The flags standing in lines, a votive offering to the Inari Shrine* in the forest in the month of February**, announces the formal coming of spring; the two men, a fisherman and a farmer, must have exchanged, when passing each other on the raised causeway, a greeting with the meaning "All's right with the world," even under the rain.

---

* The Inari God is an agricultural deity. There are many shrines dedicated to this deity is Japan; in fact there isn't a town, or village in the country without some Inari shrines. The distinguishing features of these shrines are the red *torii* leading up to them and the fox statues like guards in front of them (foxes are believed to be the servants of Inari). Annually on the first Horse Day in February a special ceremony is held in all these shrines. On that day all around the vermilion-colored *torii* banners with the name of the deity written on them are stuck into the ground, and *aburage* (fried bean-curd) said to be the favorite food of foxes and other things are placed before the shrines.

** In the days of Hiroshige the seasons were reckoned by the lunar calendar, when February corresponded to March of the Gregorian calendar.

"Azuma-no-Mori"—a   Sketch
by Hiroshige

16. Suwara. Ōban. Series: Sixty-nine Stages on the Kisokaidō.
Published by Kinjudō. About 1835-1841.

This is a view of a wayside shrine among the mountains where summer heat has been swept away by a sudden shower. The high location of the place is suggested by the faint shadow-like mountain range in the background. Among the figures the most interesting are those in silhouette, protecting themselves from the rain with rush-mats; and the humorous mountain coolies who rush into the shrine with a palanquin upside down over their heads are characteristic of Hiroshige's figures. The religious pilgrim and travelers take temporary shelter in the shrine, one of them inscribing his name on a pillar.*

The Japanese cedars that cover the shrine are submerged in dark shadow,—one of the various illustrations of Hiroshige's inventiveness.

---

* Formerly, especially in the Edo period (1615-1868), it was the custom for persons visiting the shrines to fasten their visiting cards to the pillars, walls, or ceilings of the oratories. These cards were made of paper, wood, or metal, and were called *nōsatsu* (votive cards) or *sensha* (also *senja*)-*fuda* (votive cards to a thousand shrines), *sen* (thousand) signifying here an indefinitely large number. Those who had no *nōsatsu* often wrote their names and addresses on the pillars, or walls. This practice spoiled the appearance of the oratories, and later many shrines began to provide special halls for the *nōsatsu*. The pilgrim in the picture, while seeking shelter from the rain in a roadside shrine, must have been suddenly inspired to inscribe his name on the pillar.

"Suwara"

"White Rain on Nihombashi Bridge"

17. White Rain on Nihombashi Bridge. *Ōban*. Series: Famous Views of the Eastern Capital. Published by Kikakudō. About 1833-1835.

"White Rain" is not merely a jesting word, because, lost to sight before it reaches the ground, the summer rain, white and luminous, falls perpendicularly in Japan. Whenever I see such rain in the month of July or August it reminds me of this print, "White Rain on Nihombashi Bridge," in which the red ochre of the bridge and the indigo-blue of the water are in well-composed harmony with the grey that pervades the work. I think that this is, of course, the best of Hiroshige's Nihombashi Bridges in rain or snow. The mass of the composition is finely packed. The faint cone of Mount Fuji is seen in the background through the threads of rain, and the warehouses by the river show their white panels of plaster regularly in a row. The distribution of people on the bridge is also telling.

18. Shōno. *Ōban*. Series: Fifty-three Stages on the Tōkaidō. Published by Hōeidō. About 1834.

I often wonder how an actual scene was related to the work in Hiroshige's prints. I know that there are many instances in which artists are interrupted by reality and their flight shivers and shrinks before the menace of fact. What if I insist that the pieces which related only faintly to the physiognomy of an actual place reveal themselves surprisingly new? We should find Hiroshige's greatness in the candour and freshness of his vision, not in his manner of obedience to fact, even though we admit that the support of fact was important in making the vision perform its own magic.

"Shōno," perhaps the greatest, at least one of the greatest works of this Hōeidō-edition Tōkaidō series, is an example in which the artist, for reasons not strongly influenced by reality, almost reached the apogee of his art. Someone says that there were many bamboo thickets at "Shōno" in days gone by; but I do not know why that should definitely place the scene at "Shōno." It is only a scene common by the highroad, where the sudden rain-storm made havoc among the peasants or *kago* (palanquin)-bearers. But to one asking why this work is great, I must say at once that it is the freshness of it that gives almost a feeling of being oneself. Hiroshige's integrity of vision as suggested in the work is perfect. And what a clearness in the pictorial vocabulary!

The uphill road shaded in dark-green and the bamboo thickets in the background bending under the rain form a triangle, the pictorial key-note of this composition. The subtleties of tone, particularly in the bamboo thickets, where a thousand oblique lines of rain dash down through the soft grading in greenish grey, constitute a performance no artist can achieve often in his life. You cannot fail to see how the *kago*-bearers and peasant hurry on, and how real the work is in their hurrying from nature's sudden rage.

"Shōno"

19. Sudden Shower at Ōhashi. *Ōban*. Series: Hundred Famous Views of Edo. Published by Uoei. 1856-1858.

The vertical form is used advantageously here, in the presentation of a sudden downpour on a summer day. It is more effective than the horizontal form in which Hiroshige had often treated the same subject before. It was an accidental triumph, a lucky windfall for him that what he had never anticipated was realised here by chance. The vertical form, when used wisely and freely, makes for breadth of vision and is more impressive.

We must notice in the present piece, "Sudden Shower at Ōhashi," how the artist deepened the rainy atmosphere and scent by applying a darkish orange-color to the water. It is one of the rare instances in which a vulgarized pigment used with discretion escapes being gaudy. Without the present print and a few others the series, "Meisho Edo Hyakkei" (Hundred Famous Views of Edo), would be, strictly speaking, merely pictorial caprice.

It amuses me to imagine Hiroshige producing this series of a hundred and eighteen prints. Did he ever notice, I wonder, that there was in most of them a degraded art which had no excuse for being, and which sought refuge in artistic exaggeration? Did he ever know a time when his tired mind called out more to novelty for rescue? Hiroshige must have been glad, therefore, when, as in this work, "Sudden Shower at Ōhashi," his art renewed sometimes its youthful vitality.

"Sudden Shower at Ōhashi"

And when now, more than twenty years after he had brought out the Tōkaidō series in the Hōeidō edition, he resumed the quietude of self-criticism, Hiroshige must have wondered at the changes in his art. With a sense of gratitude he must have looked upon his life and art which are equally exuberant.

20. Night Rain on Karasaki Pine Tree. Ōban. Series: Eight Views of Ōmi. Published by Hōeidō and Eisendō. About 1834.

This set was sold, as the advertisement of the first edition proves, as a "work in black and white, lightly colored." If the words were apologetic, the artist confessed that he adhered to a traditional method of light-colored painting, even to the point of imitation; and if not, he believed that, as in the landscape painting of the Chinese literary school, he could well interpret an ethereal sentiment, silence and spaces through his prints. Hiroshige produced some twenty sets of "Eight Views of Ōmi*"; among them this set published by Hōeidō and Eisendō was the first, and with its "Night Rain on Karasaki Pine Tree" and "Evening Snow on Mount Hira," is the best, the pieces cutting a figure among Hiroshige's whole work.

---

* A group of eight scenic spots on Lake Biwa near Kyōto has long been celebrated as the "Eight Views of Ōmi," Ōmi being the name of the province in which the lake is located. Included among these places of scenic beauty are Karasaki promontory where formerly the "gigantic, age-old pine tree squatted down" and Mt. Hira which overlooks the lake on the west. The pine tree mentioned above withered away later, and a young tree was planted in its place.

I do not know another work which can complete ably with this "Karasaki Pine Tree" in decorative beauty. The gigantic pine tree, a great hero of the forest kingdom, squats down with the history of a thousand years under its grey robe. The heavy vertical downpour of summer night falls on the lake water to make the little waves dance in nocturnal ringlets. The tones of light blue, grey and indigo harmonize in a unity of vision. Without this wonderful piece, and without "Evening Snow on Mount Hira," the series of "Eight Views of Ōmi" would only take a secondary place.

21. Mishima. Ōban. Series: Fifty-three Stages on the Tōkaidō.
Published by Hōeidō. About 1834.

The attractiveness of the print is to be found, of course, in the background treated as shadow in a some-what westernized method of gradation. This precedes "Miya-no-Koshi" in the series of "Sixty-nine Stages on the Kisokaidō." As this is the first time that the *bokashi zuri* (shading method), characteristic of Japanese wood-engraving, is varied with a new motif, we can excuse the artist for the resulting incongruity, since in this work the figures do not harmonize with the background as perfectly as we would wish them to. Without pointing out the forced sagacity of the artist, we should recognize his intention to create the visionary effect of a misty morning.

"Mishima"

"Hamamatsu"

22. Hamamatsu. Ōban. Series. Fifty-three Stages on the Tōkaidō.
Published by Hōeidō. About 1837.

This is the composition with a horizontal line across the lower part of the canvas, on which one big cedar tree stands, and by which figures enjoy a delightful warmth at a wood fire. The smoke of the fire is seen rising in exaggerated volume. Touched by the pastoral mood which permeates the work, we can enjoy the pleasing aspect of country life on a late autumnal day, without reference to the place, whether it be Hamamatsu or elsewhere. In work like this, the artist's temperament, simple and idyllic, reveals itself without any disguise. I am moved by the print to know how closely the village people of his day lived to the soil.

23. Numazu. Ōban. Series: Fifty-three Stages on the Tōkaidō. Published by Hōeidō. About 1834.

The travelers, father, mother and son, evidently "pilgrims to the sacred spots in the west,*" shuffle along the Tōkaidō road to seek a night's lodging at Numazu. The red mask of *tengu*, a long-nosed mountain goblin, ornamenting the sutra box that the father carries on his back, gives a grotesque impression under the gathering dusk of evening. The large moon has already appeared beyond the trees that are arranged with tasteful decorative sense; the forest on the left tightens the general composition of the work. I cannot help feeling the dreary intimacy which the work suggests in a sad undertone.

* There are in western Japan a group of thirty-three temples dedicated to Kannon, the Goddess of Mercy, which are revered by Buddhist believers as *Saikoku Sanjū-sansho Reijō* (Thirty-three Sacred Spots in the Western Provinces).

24. Miyanokoshi. Ōban. Series: Sixty-nine Stages on the Kisokaidō. Published by Kinjudō. About 1835-1841.

Here the simple wooden bridge stretches over a nondescript country river, on which a farmer's family who, I imagine, have shared the joy of a festival with kinsfolk in the distance, are now on their way home. The boy, three or four years old, is already sleeping on his father's back, while the baby is snug against the warm bosom of its mother whose head is covered, according to a country custom, with a purple-colored towel. The girl, evidently tired, shuffles along after her parents with something wrapped in a cloth. As far as we can see, this autumnal evening is lovely, while the large moon behind the trees throws a shadow in which a thatched roof and a solitary farmer make their own shadow pictures.

25. Karuizawa. Ōban. Series: Sixty-nine Stages on the Kisokaidō. Published by Kinjudō. About 1835-1841.

The present composition centers around the great Japanese cedar with its heavy leaves, half of which are lighted to pale green by the roadside wood fire smoking dramatically. By the fire a traveler is lighting his *kiseru* pipe, while the man on the pack-horse is borrowing a light from his driver. The color tone is blackish grey and enfolds everything in its shadow-like mantle.

I cannot help musing on the past, since Karuizawa, now a fashionable summer resort, was once in the rural condition pictured in this work. The mountain in the

"Miyanokoshi"

"Karuizawa"

background behind the tree is Mount Asama, Japan's best-known active volcano.

26. Mochizuki. Ōban. Series: Sixty-nine Stages on the Kisokaidō.
Published by Kinjudō. About 1835-1841.

The sheet is divided by huge pine trees which line the highway into two sections of a triangular form, one of which, more interesting than the other is a wide valley somber in dusky blue with the full moon already rising high. The figures, night travelers, some of them leading pack-horses, add to this nocturnal scene a sense of humanity which contrasts with the mood of grandeur in the silhouetted valley on the other side of the trees, where mystery silently broods.

"Mochizuki"

Whether or not it is an actual sketch of the place, the work distinguishes itself by accentuating nature through this impressive design.

27. Full-blooming Cherry Trees at Arashiyama. Ōban. Series: Famous Views of Kyōto. Published by Kawaguchi Shōzō. About 1834.

First, the special technique of the woodcut is to be seen in the indigo at the lower right, when the flowing white lines with a faint touch of blue running through express the force of water. The fire smoke leaving the raft shown in the lower part, reaches the cherry-tree in full bloom on the opposite bank, through the white space that shows the width of the river. This is a perfectly-balanced composition in which the spring of

京都名勝之内
嵐山満花

"Full-blooming Cherry Trees at Arashiyama"

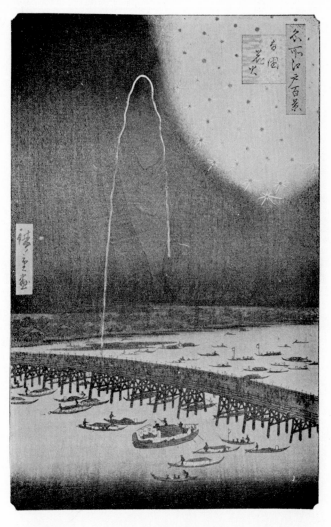

"Fireworks at Ryōgoku"

Kyōto is at its best with cherry blossoms and water that speak a human language.

28. Fireworks at Ryōgoku. *Ōban.* Series: Hundred Famous Views of Edo.
Published by Uoei. 1856-1858.

Even in the last period which includes the "Hundred Famous Views of Edo," the series of one hundred and eighteen scenes, 1856-1858, Hiroshige had, I am glad to say, not a few moments when he exclaimed:

"Let me stand at imagination's summit,
Once more think to try my flight of art!"

The present print, "Fireworks at Ryōgoku," is one of the examples in which the artist became at once audacious and young, like a sunset glow, forgetting his age to indulge in petty caprices or sad fatigue. It is true that most of the work in this series merely reports how Hiroshige was helpless against a bad Western pigment, and more than that, against people's degenerated taste at the time. But although he found himself in such unfavorable circumstances, he was, as of old, the same great appreciator of nature's eccentricity, and the same great romanticist assaulting at one focus where nature shakes off the details of environment.

I am happy to say that in this "Fireworks at Ryōgoku" and also in "Sudden Shower at Ōhashi," which has already been introduced, the vision of the artist is clear or clearer than before. The scent and atmosphere of the scenes are intense—perhaps more intense than before. While lacking, doubtless, the sensitive scrupulousness or noble transparency of the former work, the decorative picturesqueness is striking, and suggests that, as with other great artists, Hiroshige also climbed to the sun once more before his death. It is said that the last carol of a bird is its most moving.

As the subject "Fireworks at Ryōgoku" is a repetition, Hiroshige should have been thankful for the upright form of the aerial spaces with the flowery flash which was better suited than he expected.

29. Maiko-no-Hama. Ōban. Series: Views in Sixty Odd Provinces.
Published by Koshihei. 1853-1856.

Since most of the compositions of this series, "Views in Sixty Odd Provinces,*" were borrowed from various books or evolved from the artist's fancies, the work is therefore weak and flimsy. It is said that Hiroshige could not resist the forcing of his publisher, who thought only of taking advantage of his popularity. Had there been a critic to look after his art, Hiroshige might have been rescued from this mechanical labor with brushes and pigments, and been even worthier. I do not mean that every piece in the series is trash, because some of them, the present print, "Maiko-no-Hama,**" for instance, and "Hōki with Daisen Moun-

---

* From ancient times down to 1871, the chief units of local administration in Japan were the provinces. The number of these provinces was in the neighborhood of sixty-five. So the term "sixty odd provinces" was synonymous in Japanese with "Japan" or the "whole country (of Japan)."
** Maiko-no-Hama is a scenic beach in Kōbe.

"Maiko-no-hama"

tain* in Rain" and a few others, are lovely enough not to disgrace Hiroshige's reputation.

In "Maiko-no-Hama" the pine trees gesticulate, so to speak, with their peculiar arms that are painted in red ochre. I am sure that I am not the only one to feel that he hears the tropical call of the Southern Seas in this print. Red ochre is the color of the last passion of the sunset glow. I am pleased that, like stage demons with bodies painted red, the pine trees are dancing in the water. There is nothing clearer than the lyric voice heard in this print.

---

* Daisen in Hōki province (part of the present Tottori Prefecture) now constitutes the center of Daisen National Park.

LIST OF HIROSHIGE'S MORE FAMOUS SERIES

Soto to Uchi Sugata Hakkei (Eight Views with Figures, Outdoors and Indoors). Eight female-figure prints. *Ōban*. Publisher unknown. About 1823.

Gokuzaishiki Imayō Utsushi-e (Modern Images Warm-colored). Twelve female-figure prints. *Ōban* Published by Iwatoya. About 1823.

Tōto Meisho (Famous Views of the Eastern Capital). Ten prints. *Ōban*. Published by Kawaguchi Shōzō. About 1831.

Tōkaidō Gojūsan Tsugi (Fifty-three Stages on the Tōkaidō). Fifty-five prints. *Ōban*. Published by Hōeidō. 1833-1834.

"Fifty-three Stages on the Tōkaidō" in the Ezakiya edition. *Aiban*. About 1842.

"Fifty-three Stages on the Tōkaidō" in the Marusei edition. *Ōban*. 1848-1851.

Ōmi Hakkei (Eight Views of Ōmi). Eight prints. *Ōban*. Published by Hōeidō and Eisendō. About 1834.

Kyōto Meisho (Famous Views of Kyōto). Ten prints. *Ōban*. Published by Kawaguchi Shōzō. About 1834.

Kanazawa Hakkei (Eight Views of Kanazawa). Eight

prints. *Ōban*. Published by Koshihei. About 1836.

Wakan Rōeishū (Recitative Poems of Japan and China). Seven prints. *Ōban*. Published by Jokin. About 1839.

Edo Kinkō Hakkei (Eight Views of Environs of Edo). Eight prints. *Ōban*. Published by Kikakudō. About 1838.

Honchō Meisho (Famous Views of Japan). Fifteen prints. *Ōban*. Published by Shōgendō. About 1832.

Kisokaidō Rokujū-ku Tsugi (Sixty-nine Stages on the Kisokaidō). Forty-seven prints. *Ōban*. Published by Kinjudō. About 1835-1841.

Tōto Meisho (Famous Views of the Eastern Capital). About twenty prints. *Ōban*. Published by Kikakudō. About 1833-1835.

Edo Hyakkei (Hundred Famous Views of Edo). One hundred and eighteen prints. *Ōban*. Published by Uoei. 1856-1858.

Rokujū Yoshū Meisho Zu-e (Views in Sixty Odd Provinces). Sixty-eight prints. *Ōban*. Published by Koshihei 1853-1856.

BIBLIOGRAPHY

Amsden (Dora) and Happer (J.S.): *The Heritage of Hiroshige.* San Francisco, 1912.

Fenollosa, Mary McNeil: *Hiroshige, the Artist of Mist, Snow and Rain.* San Francisco, 1901.

Kojima, Usui: *Ukiyo-e to Fūkeiga* (*Ukiyo-e* and Landscapes). Tōkyō, 1914.

Kimura, Sōhachi: *Hiroshige.* Tōkyō, 1927.

Noguchi, Yone: *Hiroshige.* Tōkyō, Kyōbunkan, 1934.

Strange, Edward F.: *Colour Prints of Hiroshige.* London, 1925.

Uchida, Minoru: *Hiroshige.* Tōkyō, 1930.

Watanabe, Shōzaburō: *Catalogue of the Memorial Exhibition of Hiroshige's Works on the 60th Anniversary of his Death.* Tōkyō, 1918.

INDEX

TOYOKUNI - actors

HOKUSAI - landscape "36 view of Mt. Fuji"